HOME WORK

Date	Assignment	Signature

KB086806

UNIT COMPONENTS

• KEY PATTERNS

Key words and key patterns are presented in context.
Students can role-play the conversation used in the cartoon.

• VOCABULARY

Vocabulary words can be used immediately through activities related to pattern sentences.

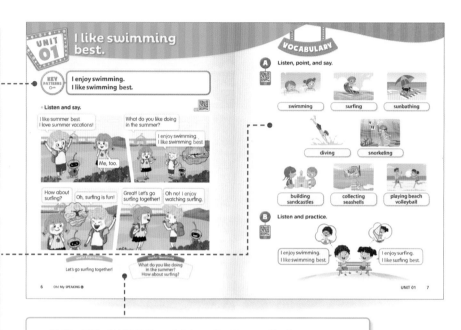

• USEFUL EXPRESSIONS & QUESTIONS

A variety of particularly useful expressions from the dialogues in the cartoons allow students to develop their speaking skills.

• KEY PATTERN PRACTICE

Repeating sentences with key patterns helps students to naturally remember what they have learned.

• LISTEN AND SPEAK

Substituting words in key patterns in a combined listening and speaking activity assists students to build their speaking fluency.

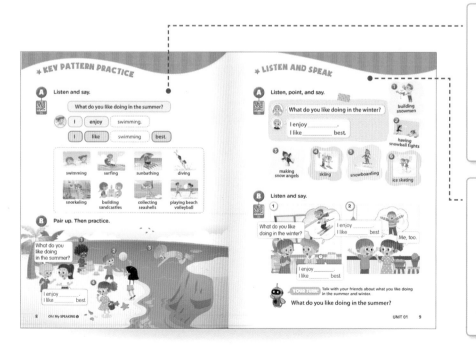

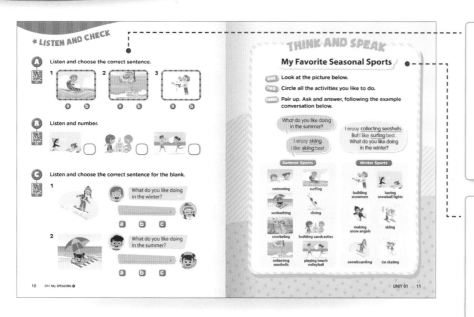

• LISTEN AND CHECK

Listening practice gets students to relate the key sentences to the pictures and to learn how to use the right sentences in the conversation.

• THINK AND SPEAK

A fun and educational communication game gets students to practice key sentences repeatedly.

REVIEW TEST

Word reviews and a variety of speaking and listening activities help students recall and further practice key words and key patterns from previous units.

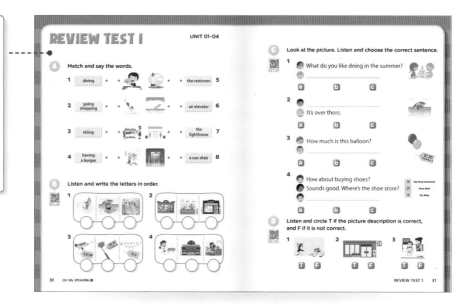

WORKBOOK

Various writing, listening, and speaking exercises allow students to review key words and key patterns learned in the Student Book.

CONTENTS

UNIT 01
I like swimming best.

I enjoy swimming.
I like swimming best.

Listen and say.

I like summer best.
I love summer vacations!

What do you like doing in the summer?

I enjoy swimming.
I like swimming best.

Me, too.

How about surfing?

Oh, surfing is fun!

Great! Let's go surfing together!

Oh no! I enjoy watching surfing.

Useful Expression

Let's go surfing together!

Useful Questions

What do you like doing in the summer?
How about surfing?

VOCABULARY

A Listen, point, and say.

swimming

surfing

sunbathing

diving

snorkeling

building sandcastles

collecting seashells

playing beach volleyball

B Listen and practice.

I enjoy swimming.
I like swimming best.

I enjoy surfing.
I like surfing best.

★ KEY PATTERN PRACTICE

 A   **Listen and say.**

> **What do you like doing in the summer?**

I	enjoy	swimming.	
I	like	swimming	best.

swimming   surfing   sunbathing   diving

snorkeling   building   collecting   playing beach
                sandcastles   seashells   volleyball

B   **Pair up. Then practice.**

What do you
like doing
in the summer?

I enjoy _____.
I like _____ best.

★ LISTEN AND SPEAK

A Listen, point, and say.

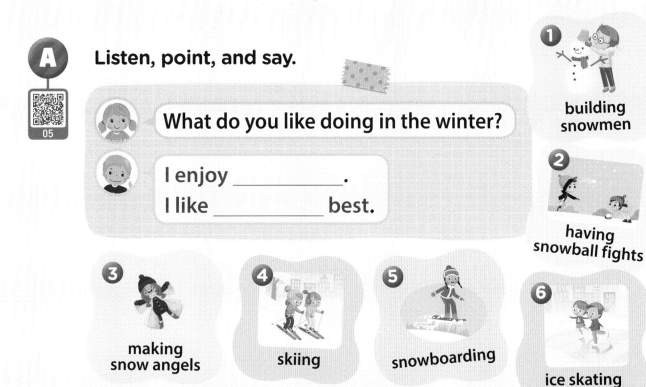

What do you like doing in the winter?

I enjoy _____.
I like _____ best.

1 building snowmen

2 having snowball fights

3 making snow angels

4 skiing

5 snowboarding

6 ice skating

B Listen and say.

1

What do you like doing in the winter?

I enjoy _____.
I like _____ best.

2

I enjoy _____.
I like _____ best.

Me, too.

YOUR TURN! Talk with your friends about what you like doing in the summer and winter.

What do you like doing in the summer?

★ LISTEN AND CHECK

A Listen and choose the correct sentence.

1
ⓐ ⓑ

2
ⓐ ⓑ

3
ⓐ ⓑ

B   Listen and number.

C   Listen and choose the correct sentence for the blank.

1

 What do you like doing in the winter?

 _____.

 a   b   c

2

 What do you like doing in the summer?

 _____.

 a   b   c

THINK AND SPEAK

My Favorite Seasonal Sports

ONE Look at the picture below.

TWO Circle all the activities you like to do.

THREE Pair up. Ask and answer, following the example conversation below.

> What do you like doing in the summer?

> I enjoy skiing.
> I like skiing best.

> I enjoy collecting seashells.
> But I like surfing best.
> What do you like doing in the winter?

Summer Sports

swimming

surfing

sunbathing

diving

snorkeling

building sandcastles

collecting seashells

playing beach volleyball

Winter Sports

building snowmen

having snowball fights

making snow angels

skiing

snowboarding

ice skating

Where can I find the restroom?

KEY PATTERNS

Where can I find **the restroom**?
I'm looking for **a charging station**.

I'm = I am

Listen and say.

Excuse me. Where can I find the restroom?

It's around the corner.

Thank you.

Oh, my battery is low!

You should recharge it.

Excuse me. I'm looking for a charging station.

It's over there.

Thank you.

Wacky, where are you?

Jack, I'm here. I'm full.

Useful Expressions

My battery is low!
I'm here.

Useful Question

Where are you?

VOCABULARY

A Listen, point, and say.

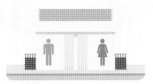

the restroom

a convenience store

a gift shop

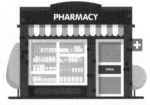

a pharmacy

an elevator

a cafe

a fast food restaurant

the information center

the lost-and-found center

B Listen and practice.

Excuse me. Where can I find the restroom?

It's around the corner.

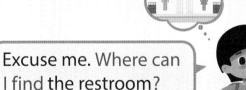

★ KEY PATTERN PRACTICE

 Listen and say.

I'm **looking for** the restroom.

It's around the corner.

Where **can** **I** **find** the restroom?

It's over there.

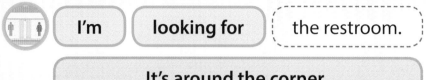

the restroom

a convenience store

a gift shop

a pharmacy

an elevator

a cafe

a fast food restaurant

the information center

the lost-and-found center

 **Pair up. Then practice.**

Excuse me. I'm looking for _____.

It's around the corner.

Excuse me. Where can I find _____?

It's over there.

★ LISTEN AND SPEAK

 A **Listen, point, and say.**

I'm looking for _____.

It's around the corner.

Where can I find _____?

It's over there.

1

a hammock

2

a sun chair

3

a beach umbrella

4

the boardwalk

5

the lighthouse

6

a palm tree

 B **Listen and say.**

1

Excuse me. I'm looking for _____.

It's over there.

2

Excuse me. Where can I find _____?

It's around the corner.

YOUR TURN! Ask and answer about where to find things and places.

Where can I find the restroom?

★ LISTEN AND CHECK

A Listen and choose the correct sentence.

1
    a   **b**

2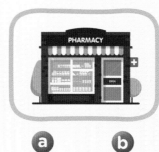
    a   **b**

3
    a   **b**

B Listen and number.

C Listen and check T for True or F for False.

1 Wacky was looking for a fast food restaurant.

          T   **F**

2 Jack found Wacky at a charging station.

          T   **F**

THINK AND SPEAK

I'm looking for the restroom.

ONE Pair up. Look at the map below.

TWO Ask and answer using the vocabulary word in the box, following the example conversation below.

> next to   between A and B   across the street from

Excuse me. I'm looking for the restroom.

It's next to the lost-and-found center.

Excuse me. Where can I find the convenience store?

It's across the street from the gift shop.

the hotel

the pharmacy

the information center

the cafe

the lighthouse

the gift shop

the convenience store

You are here

the lost-and-found center

the restroom

UNIT 03

How much is this?

How much is this/that drone?
It's $100. / It's $40 for one and $70 for two.

• **Listen and say.**

Wacky, I want a new drone. Can you help me find a good one?

Sure.

I like the red one. How much is this?

It's $100.

It's too expensive! I only have $30. How much is that drone?

It's $40 for one and $70 for two.

If you clean your room, I'll give you $10.

Yay! I'll clean my room right now!

Useful Expression

It's too expensive!

Useful Question

Can you help me find a good one?

VOCABULARY

A Listen, point, and say.

$40
($70 for 2)

drone

$98.86
($190 for 2)

cell phone

$10.99
($16 for 2)

mini fan

$29.30
($50 for 2)

wireless mic

$139.99
($260 for 2)

laptop

$9.48
($18 for 2)

selfie stick

60 sixty **70** seventy **80** eighty **90** ninety **100** hundred

B Listen and practice.

How much is this drone?

$40
($70 for 2)

It's $40.

It's $40 for one and $70 for two.

★ KEY PATTERN PRACTICE

A Listen and say.

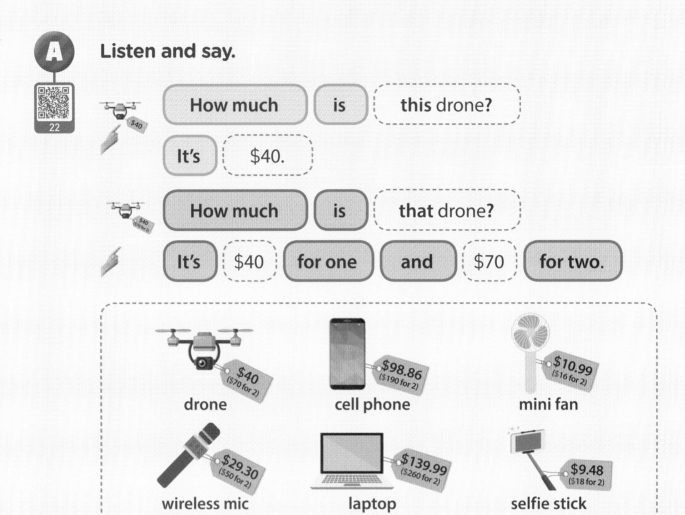

| How much | is | **this** drone? |

| It's | $40. |

| How much | is | **that** drone? |

| It's | $40 | for one | and | $70 | for two. |

drone — $40 ($70 for 2)

cell phone — $98.86 ($190 for 2)

mini fan — $10.99 ($16 for 2)

wireless mic — $29.30 ($50 for 2)

laptop — $139.99 ($260 for 2)

selfie stick — $9.48 ($18 for 2)

B Pair up. Then practice.

How much is this _____?

How much is that _____?

It's _____.

It's _____ for one and _____ for two.

$78

$99.99

$15.30 ($25 for 2)

$12 ($20 for 2)

LISTEN AND SPEAK

A Listen, point, and say.

How much is this _____?

It's _____.

How much is that _____?

It's _____ for one and _____ for two.

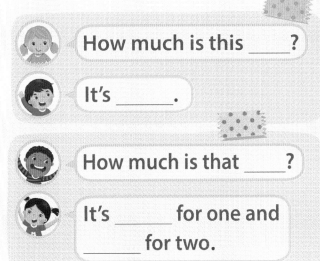

1 $3.50 ($5 for 2)
birthday card

2 $1.50 ($2.40 for 2)
balloon

3 $4.98 ($8 for 2)
candle

4 $12.99 ($20 for 2)
banner

5 $26.54 ($45 for 2)
mask

6 $22.99 ($36 for 2)
water gun

B Listen and say.

1 How much is this _____?

It's _____.

$25 $26

2 How much is that _____?

$3.50 ($6 for 2)

It's _____ for one and _____ for two.

CARDS

YOUR TURN! Talk about the prices of the things you have.

How much is this?

★ LISTEN AND CHECK

A Listen and choose the correct sentence.

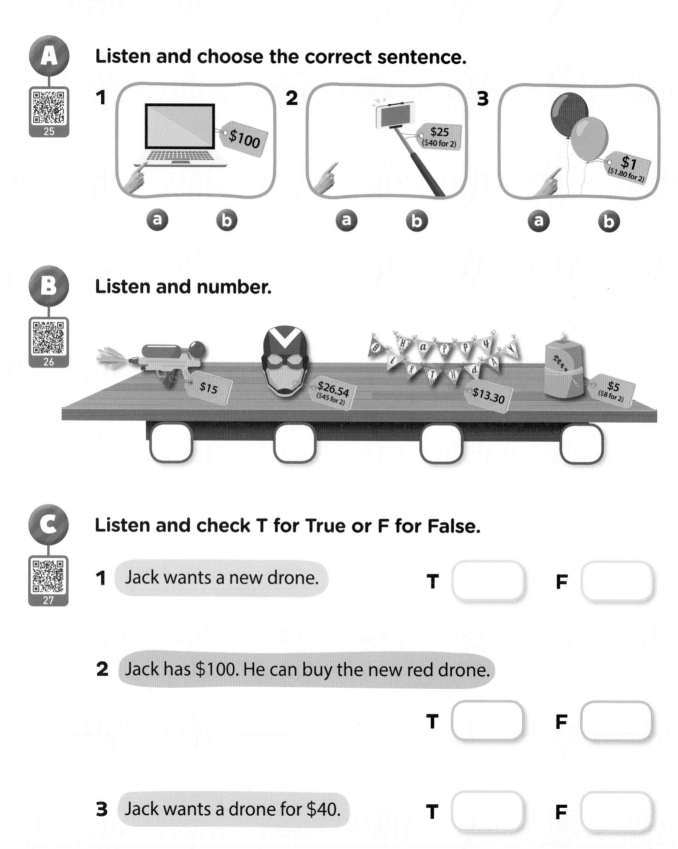

1
$100

ⓐ   ⓑ

2
$25
($40 for 2)

ⓐ   ⓑ

3
$1
($1.80 for 2)

ⓐ   ⓑ

B Listen and number.

$15

$26.54
($45 for 2)

$13.30

$5
($8 for 2)

C Listen and check T for True or F for False.

1 Jack wants a new drone.   T ⬚   F ⬚

2 Jack has $100. He can buy the new red drone.

T ⬚   F ⬚

3 Jack wants a drone for $40.   T ⬚   F ⬚

What would you choose to buy?

ONE You have only $50 to decorate for the birthday party.

TWO Pair up. Choose the items you want. Stay within your budget.

THREE Role-play with your friend as a customer and a clerk.

How much is this <u>balloon</u>?

It's <u>$1.50</u> for one and <u>$2.40</u> for two.

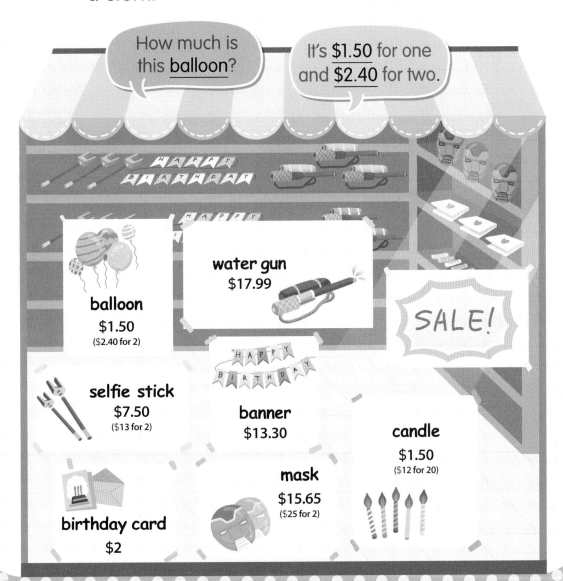

water gun
$17.99

balloon
$1.50
($2.40 for 2)

SALE!

selfie stick
$7.50
($13 for 2)

banner
$13.30

candle
$1.50
($12 for 20)

mask
$15.65
($25 for 2)

birthday card
$2

UNIT 04

How about playing table tennis?

Listen and say.

Hi, Jack. How about playing table tennis tomorrow?

Sounds good.

How about having lunch before the game?

Okay. Where do you want to meet?

Let's meet at King's Burger.

Sure. Where is it?

It's on the second floor of that building.

Okay, I see it. See you there at 12.

Useful Expressions

Sounds good.
See you there at 12.

Useful Questions

Where do you want to meet?
Where is it?

VOCABULARY

A Listen, point, and say.

playing table tennis

going to the theater

having a burger

going shopping

buying a present

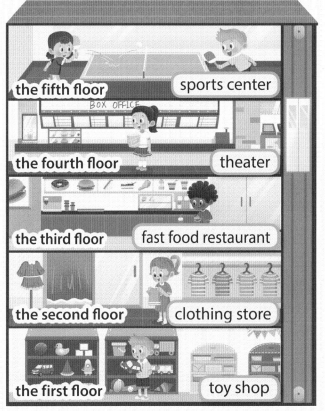

the fifth floor — sports center

the fourth floor — theater

the third floor — fast food restaurant

the second floor — clothing store

the first floor — toy shop

B Listen and practice.

How about playing table tennis?

It's on the fifth floor.

Okay. Where's the sports center?

★ KEY PATTERN PRACTICE

A **Listen and say.**

31

How about | playing table tennis?

Sounds good. Where's the sports center?

It's **on** | **the fifth floor.**

playing table tennis   going to the theater   having a burger

going shopping   buying a present

the fifth floor   sports center

the fourth floor   theater

the third floor   fast food restaurant

the second floor   clothing store

the first floor   toy shop

B **Pair up. Then practice.**

1. How about _____?

2. Okay.

3. Where's the _____?

4. It's on the _____ floor.

★ LISTEN AND SPEAK

A  Listen, point, and say.

How about _____ ?

Sounds good.
Where's the _____ ?

It's on the _____ floor.

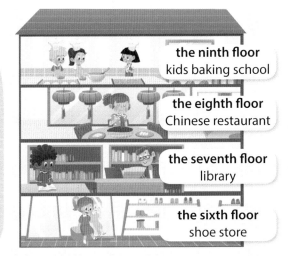

the ninth floor
kids baking school

the eighth floor
Chinese restaurant

the seventh floor
library

the sixth floor
shoe store

1
learning baking

2 CHINESE FOOD
having Chinese food

3 LIBRARY
reading books

4
buying shoes

B Listen and say.

1

How about _____ ?

Sounds good.

2

Where's the Chinese restaurant?

9F	Chinese Restaura
8F	Shoe Store
7F	Library

It's on the _____ floor.

 **YOUR TURN!** Suggest doing an activity together to your friend.

How about having lunch together?

★ LISTEN AND CHECK

A Listen and choose the correct sentence.

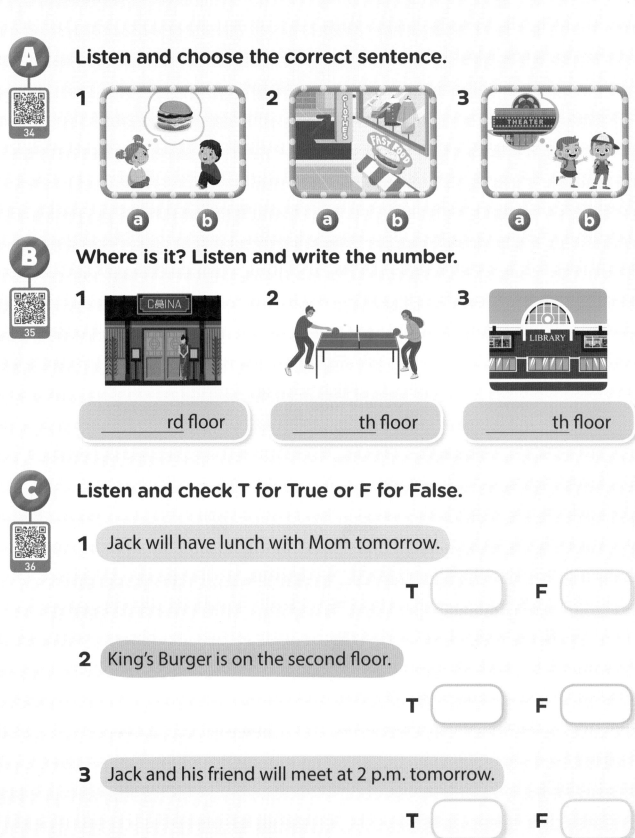

1
ⓐ ⓑ

2
ⓐ ⓑ

3
ⓐ ⓑ

B Where is it? Listen and write the number.

1
_____ rd floor

2
_____ th floor

3
_____ th floor

C Listen and check T for True or F for False.

1 Jack will have lunch with Mom tomorrow.

T ⬜ F ⬜

2 King's Burger is on the second floor.

T ⬜ F ⬜

3 Jack and his friend will meet at 2 p.m. tomorrow.

T ⬜ F ⬜

THINK AND SPEAK

Making Plans with Your Friends

ONE Look at the floor plan of the building below.

TWO Pair up and choose an activity from the box.

THREE Role-play with your partners, following the example below.

Activity Box

playing table tennis	having a burger	going to the theater
going shopping	having Chinese food	buying a present
buying shoes	reading books	learning baking

9F	a kids baking school
8F	a theater
7F	a library
6F	a sports center
5F	a Chinese restaurant
4F	a toy shop
3F	a clothing store
2F	a fast food restaurant
1F	a shoe store

How about playing table tennis?

Okay. Is there a sports center?

Sure. It's on the sixth floor.

REVIEW TEST I

A Match and say the words.

1 diving

2 going shopping

3 skiing

4 having a burger

5 the restroom

6 an elevator

7 the lighthouse

8 a sun chair

B Listen and write the letters in order.

1

2

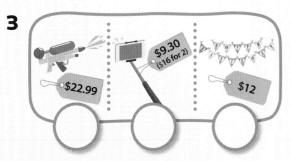

3

$22.99 $9.30 ($16 for 2) $12

4

C Look at the picture. Listen and choose the correct sentence.

1

What do you like doing in the summer?

_____

a   b   c

2

_____

It's over there.

a   b   c

3

How much is this balloon?

_____

a   b   c

$1.50
($2.40 for 2)

4

How about buying shoes?

Sounds good. Where's the shoe store?

_____

a   b   c

3F	fast food restaurant
2F	shoe store
1F	toy shop

D Listen and circle T if the picture description is correct, and F if it is not correct.

1

T   F

2

T   F

3

T   F

E **Prepare birthday gifts for your friend.**

STEP I Choose and write the correct words for each blank.

> How much is that water gun

> It's $8

> I only have $30

> is this selfie stick

I want to buy a birthday gift for Kevin.
Can you help me?

Sure. How much money do you have?

$30

_____.

What do you want to buy?

I want to buy a selfie stick. How much
_____?

_____.

$8

_____?

It's $13 for one and $20 for two.

$13
($20 for 2)

I'll take a selfie stick and two water guns.

STEP 2 You have only $30. Choose the gift items you want. Stay within your budget. Then write the chosen items in the gift box.

$3
($5 for 2)

$11.99

$20
($30 for 2)

$9
($15 for 2)

$2

$15
($25 for 2)

Write your gifts here!

STEP 3 What would you choose to buy for your friend's birthday? You can choose from the box in Step 2. Write and talk about them with your partner.

I want to buy birthday gifts for my friend _____.
(name)

I only have _____.
(money)

I want to buy _____ and _____.

_____ is _____.
(item)   (price)

_____ is _____ for one and
(item)   (price)

_____ for two.

I hope he/she will like my gifts.

Can I bring my dog?

Can you come to my birthday party?
Can I bring my dog?

Listen and say.

Can you come to my birthday party on Saturday?

Sure. Thanks.

Can I bring my dog?

Hold on. Let me ask my mom.

Mom, can Jack bring his dog?

Sure.

You can bring your dog.

Great! See you on Saturday.

Useful Expressions

Hold on.
Let me ask my mom.

Useful Question

Can Jack bring his dog?

A Listen, point, and say.

my birthday party

my house

the concert

the picnic

the play

dog

friend

little brother

B Listen and practice.

Can you come to my birthday party?

Sure. Can I bring my dog?

★ KEY PATTERN PRACTICE

A Listen and say.

43

Can | you | come | to | my birthday party?

Can | I | bring | my | dog?

| my birthday party | my house | the concert | the picnic |

| the play | dog | friend | little brother |

B Pair up. Then practice.

Can you come to _____ on Saturday?

Sure. Can I bring my _____?

Okay. See you on Saturday.

1 friend

2 little brother

3 dog

4 friend

LISTEN AND SPEAK

A Listen, point, and say.

Can you come to _____?

Sure. Can I bring my _____?

Of course. See you on Saturday.

camera

hat

1 the school festival

2 the amusement park

3 the talent show

4 the baseball game

B Listen and say.

1

Can you come to _____?

Sure. Thanks.

2

Can you come to _____?

Sure. Can I bring my _____?

Okay.

YOUR TURN! Invite your friend to your birthday party.

Can you come to my birthday party?

★ LISTEN AND CHECK

A Listen and choose the correct sentence.

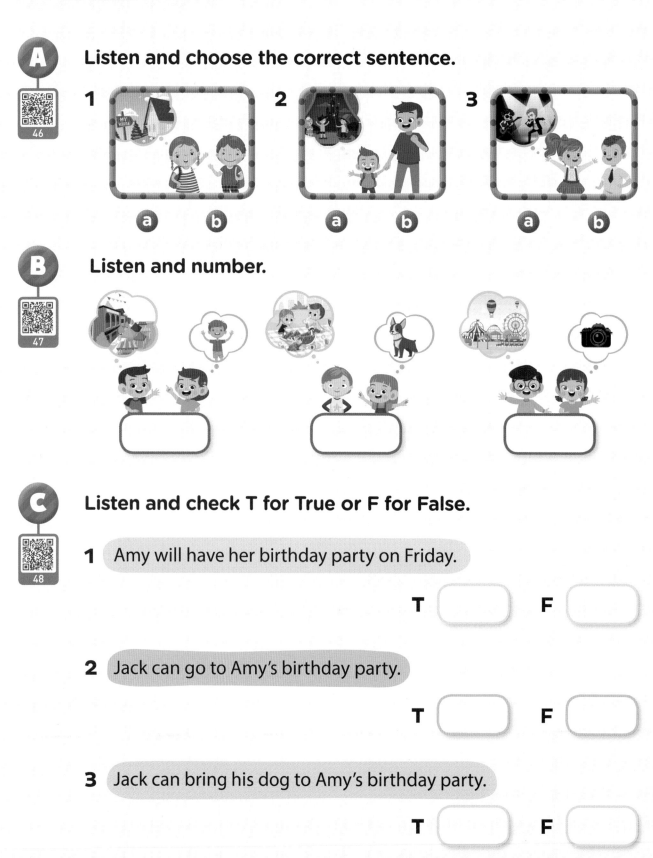

1
a   b

2
a   b

3
a   b

B Listen and number.

C Listen and check T for True or F for False.

1   Amy will have her birthday party on Friday.

T ⬜   F ⬜

2   Jack can go to Amy's birthday party.

T ⬜   F ⬜

3   Jack can bring his dog to Amy's birthday party.

T ⬜   F ⬜

Exciting Events

ONE Look at the posters below.

TWO Pair up. Ask questions and provide answers, following the example conversation below.

Can you come to the talent show?

Sure. Can I bring my friend?

Yes, you can.

Can you come to the play?

Sure. Can I bring my dog?

No, you can't. I'm sorry.

NOTICE

The Concert
Date: Wednesday, September 10th
Time: 6 pm
Place: CEDU Concert Hall

THE FALL FESTIVAL
Date: Friday, October 23rd
Time: 5:00 pm – 7:30 pm
Place: CEDU Elementary

The Talent Show
Date: Saturday, May 7th
Time: 3 pm
Place: CEDU Theater

The Little Mermaid
Date: November 15 – 18
Time: 1 pm – 3 pm
4 pm – 6 pm
Place: CEDU Theater

The Kids Baseball Game
Date: November 15 – 18
Time: 1 pm – 3 pm
4 pm – 6 pm
Place: CEDU Playground

UNIT 06

You must be quiet in here.

You must **be quiet in here.**
You must **not shout in here.**

Listen and say.

Wow, those robots are amazing!

It's so noisy in here.

I want to take pictures.

Excuse me. You must not take pictures in here.

Pardon? What did you say?

You must not shout in here.

I can't hear you!

You must be quiet in here!

Useful Expression

I can't hear you!

Useful Questions

Pardon?
What did you say?

VOCABULARY

Listen, point, and say.

You must

be quiet

be on time

be careful

be polite

You must not

shout

be late

run around

be rude

B Listen and practice.

You must be quiet.

You must not shout.

★ KEY PATTERN PRACTICE

A **Listen and say.**

52

You | must | be quiet.

You | must | not | shout.

You must

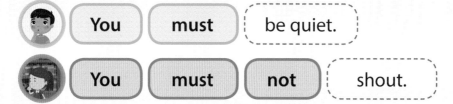

| be quiet | be on time | be careful | be polite |

You must not

| shout | be late | run around | be rude |

B **Pair up. Then practice.**

You must _____.

You must not _____.

★ LISTEN AND SPEAK

 A **Listen, point, and say.**

 You must _____ .   You must not _____ .

You must

1 stop at the red light

3 wait in line

5 get enough sleep

You must not

2 cross the street at the red light

4 cut in line

6 stay up late

 B **Listen and say. What would you say to them?**

1 You must not
_____ .

2 You must _____
at the red light.

 YOUR TURN! Ask your friend what he/she must and must not do.

You must be quiet in here.

★ LISTEN AND CHECK

A Listen and choose the correct sentence.

1  a b

2 a b

3 a b

B Listen and number.

C Listen and check T for True or F for False.

1 It's quiet in the exhibit hall.   T   F

2 Jack can take pictures in the exhibit hall.

T   F

3 Jack must not shout in the exhibit hall.

T   F

THINK AND SPEAK

You must and you must not...

ONE Pair up.

TWO Role-play with your partners, following the example conversation below. Say the sentence using "You must _____." or "You must not _____."

1 in the library

Hey! Come over here!

You must **be quiet** in the library.

2 in the theater

I want to take pictures.

You must not _____ in here.

3 at the crosswalk STOP

Can I cross the street?

No. You must _____ _____.

4 in class DON'T BE LATE

I'm sorry. I'm late.

You must not _____.

5 on the wet floor CAUTION

Uh oh.

You must _____ on the wet floor.

6 in the art museum

Hey, catch me!

You must not _____ in here.

A coat is warmer than a jacket.

KEY PATTERNS

A coat is warmer than **a jacket.**
A car is more comfortable than **a train.**

Listen and say.

Yay! We're going to take a trip.

It's cold. Put on a coat. A coat is warmer than a jacket.

Let's take the train.

No. I think a car is more comfortable than a train.

A train is faster than a car.

Is that a hill or a mountain?

That's a mountain. A mountain is higher than a hill.

Yum! I'll have a sandwich. This sandwich is bigger than that hot dog.

Slow down! Chew it well.

Useful Expressions

Put on a coat.
Slow down! Chew it well.

Useful Question

Is that a hill or a mountain?

VOCABULARY

Listen, point, and say.

a jacket / a coat
warm – warmer

a hill / a mountain
high – higher

 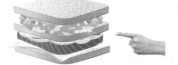

that hot dog / this sandwich
big – bigger

silver / gold
expensive – more expensive

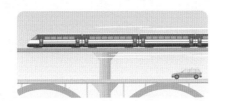

a car / a train
fast – faster

a train / a car
comfortable – more comfortable

B **Listen and practice.**

A coat is warmer than a jacket.

A car is more comfortable than a train.

★ KEY PATTERN PRACTICE

A   Listen and say.

61

A coat — is — warmer — than — a jacket.

Gold — is — more expensive — than — silver.

a jacket / a coat
warm – warmer

a hill / a mountain
high – higher

that hot dog / this sandwich
big – bigger

silver / gold
expensive –
more expensive

a car / a train
fast – faster

a train / a car
comfortable –
more comfortable

B   Pair up. Look and practice.

_____ is _____ than _____.

_____ is more _____ than _____.

❶

❷

❸

❹

★ LISTEN AND SPEAK

A   Listen, point, and say.

62

_____ is (more) _____ than _____.

1

a river / a lake
small – smaller

2

a rock / a feather
light – lighter

3

a bear / an elephant
heavy – heavier

4

English / math
difficult – more difficult

B   Listen and say.

63

1

An elephant is
_____ than a bear.
(heavy)

2

Math is _____
_____ than English.
(difficult)

YOUR TURN! Compare the two items using comparative forms.

Which one is faster?

★ LISTEN AND CHECK

A Listen and choose the correct sentence.

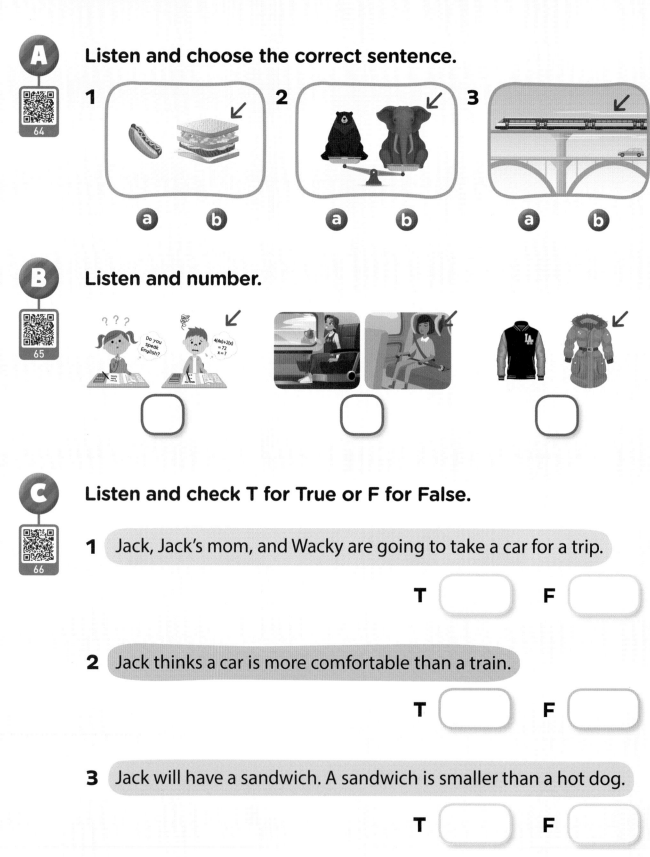

1   a   b

2   a   b

3   a   b

B Listen and number.

C Listen and check T for True or F for False.

1 Jack, Jack's mom, and Wacky are going to take a car for a trip.

T   F

2 Jack thinks a car is more comfortable than a train.

T   F

3 Jack will have a sandwich. A sandwich is smaller than a hot dog.

T   F

Comparative Board Game

 Pair up.

 Roll the die and play the game. When you land on a green square, make a comparative sentence using the adjective and two things shown on the square.

light a rock, a feather	A feather is lighter than a rock.	A car is more comfortable than a train.	**comfortable** a train, a car

Move 2 squares backward	**expensive** silver, gold	Restart	**difficult** English, math	**Finish**
Lose a Chance!				
light a rock, a feather				
heavy a bear, an elephant	Lose a Chance!	**high** a hill, a mountain	**comfortable** a train, a car	Move 2 squares forward
				small a river, a lake
				big a dog, an elephant
Start →	**warm** a jacket, a coat	**fast** a car, a train	Move 3 squares forward	Restart

She's the tallest member.

KEY PATTERNS

She's the tallest member.
(I think) he's the most
handsome member.

She's = She is
He's = He is

Listen and say.

67

I like BGS! They're my most favorite group.

They're the most popular singing group in the world!

Oh, I didn't know that.

BGS? Are they singers?

Look! She's the tallest member.

Wow, she's really tall!

Who's the most handsome member?

I think he's the most handsome member.

Useful Expression
I didn't know that.

Useful Questions
Are they singers?
Who's the most handsome member?

VOCABULARY

A Listen, point, and say.

tall – taller – the tallest
woman

old – older – the oldest
man

young – younger – the youngest
child

strong – stronger – the strongest
boy

funny – funnier – the funniest
girl

popular – more popular – the most popular
singer

B Listen and practice.

She's the tallest member.

I think he's the most popular member.

smart   kind   active
cheerful   friendly   brave

★ KEY PATTERN PRACTICE

A Listen and say.

| She's/He's | **the tallest** | woman/man | among them. |

| I think | he's/she's | **the most popular** | singer |

among them.

tall – taller – the tallest
woman

old – older – the oldest
man

young – younger –
the youngest
child

strong – stronger – the strongest
boy

funny – funnier – the funniest
girl

popular – more popular –
the most popular
Singer

B Pair up. Then practice.

Who's the
_____?

She's the
_____.

① woman ② girl ▪ singer ④ man ③

Who's the (most)
_____ _____?

I think he's
the (most)
_____.

★ LISTEN AND SPEAK

A Listen, point, and say.

👩 **This** is the (most) _____ _____.

👦 **It's** the (most) _____ _____.

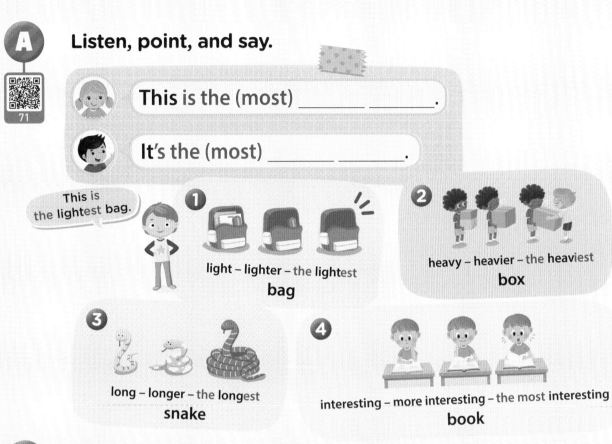

This is the lightest bag.

① light – lighter – the lightest
bag

② heavy – heavier – the heaviest
box

③ long – longer – the longest
snake

④ interesting – more interesting – the most interesting
book

B Listen and say.

① Ugh! This is the _____ bag.

This is the _____ bag.

② This is the _____ snake!

Oh, I'm scared.

 YOUR TURN! Compare and talk about the members.

Who's your most favorite singing group?

★ LISTEN AND CHECK

A Listen and choose the correct sentence.

73

1
ⓐ ⓑ

2
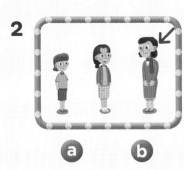
ⓐ ⓑ

3

ⓐ ⓑ

B Listen and number.

74

C Listen and check T for True or F for False.

75

1 BGS is Amy's most favorite group.　　T ☐　　F ☐

2 Jack already knew about BGS.　　T ☐　　F ☐

3 BGS is an all-boy band.　　T ☐　　F ☐

THINK AND SPEAK

Let's compare.

ONE Look at the pictures of the three children and the sentences below.

TWO Fill in the blanks.

THREE Pair up. Compare and share your own opinions.

Ken   Judy   Dave

Dave   Judy   Ken

Dave   Judy   Ken

Dave   Judy   Ken

Comparative

1. Dave is _____ than Ken.
   (young)

2. Judy is _____ than Dave.
   (old)

3. Ken is _____ than Judy.
   (tall)

Superlative

1. Dave is the _____ boy.
   (popular)

2. Ken is the _____ boy.
   (tall)

3. Ken is the _____ boy.
   (strong)

REVIEW TEST 2

A. Match and say the words.

1 the play

2 the picnic

3 cut in line

4 run around

5 bigger

6 faster

7 the strongest

8 the tallest

B. Listen and write the letters in order.

1

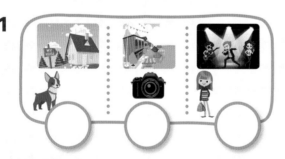

2

3

4

C Look at the picture. Listen and choose the correct sentence.

1

 Can you come to the baseball game?

 _____

Sure, you can.

a   b   c

2

I can't hear you!

_____

a   b   c

3

Let's take the train.

No. _____

a   b   c

4

_____

Wow! It's very light.

a   b   c

D Listen and circle T if the picture description is correct, and F if it is not correct.

1

T   F

2

T   F

3

T   F

REVIEW TEST 2

E Talk about your most favorite singer.

STEP 1 Choose and write the correct words for each blank.

He's the youngest member

the most popular group

longer

I think he's the most handsome member

the tallest

I like BGS. They're _____ in the world.

I don't know them. Can you tell me about them?

Look at this picture. My favorite member is Kevin. He's _____ member.

Does he have long hair?

Yes. His hair is _____ than Kelly's, but shorter than Peter's hair.

I see. How old is Kevin?

He's 17. _____. Peter and Kelly are older than him.

Wow! He's handsome.

That's right. _____!

STEP 2 There is more information about Kevin. Check the right picture about Kevin.

Which one is Kevin?

Kevin is the most popular member.

Kevin's shoes are the biggest.

Kevin is stronger than Kelly, but weaker than Peter.

Kevin's eyes are bigger than Peter's, but smaller than Kelly's.

STEP 3 Think about your most favorite singer. Choose words from the box that best describe him or her. Then talk about him or her with your friends.

> young   tall   popular   funny

This is my most favorite group _____.
(group name)

My most favorite member is _____.
(name)

He's/She's the _____ member in the group.

And I think he's/she's the _____ member

in the group. I like him/her so much!

SCOPE & SEQUENCE

UNIT 01 I like swimming best.

Key Patterns	Vocabulary	Useful Expression	Goals
I enjoy **swimming**. I like **swimming** best.	swimming / surfing / sunbathing / diving / snorkeling / building sandcastles / collecting seashells / playing beach volleyball / building snowmen / having snowball fights / making snow angels / skiing / snowboarding / ice skating	Let's go surfing together! **Useful Questions** What do you like doing in the summer? How about surfing?	• Talking about favorite seasonal activities • Talking about what you like doing • Emphasizing how much you like doing it ● Theme Seasonal activities

UNIT 02 Where can I find the restroom?

Key Patterns	Vocabulary	Useful Expressions	Goals
Where can I find **the restroom?** I'm looking for **a charging station.**	the restroom / a convenience store / a gift shop / a pharmacy / an elevator / a cafe / a fast food restaurant / the information center / the lost-and-found center / a hammock / a sun chair / a beach umbrella / the boardwalk / the lighthouse / a palm tree	My battery is low! I'm here. **Useful Question** Where are you?	• Talking about places • Talking about what you are looking for ● Theme Places and things that you are looking for

UNIT 03 How much is this?

Key Patterns	Vocabulary	Useful Expression	Goals
How much is this/ that **drone?** It's $100. It's $40 for one and $70 for two.	drone / cell phone / mini fan / wireless mic / laptop / selfie stick / sixty / seventy / eighty / ninety / hundred / birthday card / balloon / candle / banner / mask / water gun	It's too expensive! **Useful Question** Can you help me find a good one?	• Talking about prices • Learning numbers sixty to a hundred • Understanding sales terms ● Theme Prices

UNIT 04 How about playing table tennis?

Key Patterns	Vocabulary	Useful Expressions	Goals
How about **playing table tennis?** It's on the **second** floor.	playing table tennis / going to the theater / having a burger / going shopping / buying a present / sports center / theater / fast food restaurant / clothing store / toy shop / learning baking / having Chinese food / reading books / buying shoes / kids baking school / Chinese restaurant / library / shoe store / first / second / third / fourth / fifth / sixth / seventh / eighth / ninth	Sounds good. See you there at 12. **Useful Questions** Where do you want to meet? Where is it?	• Making a suggestion • Making a plan to meet a friend • Using ordinal numbers ● Theme Suggestion

REVIEW TEST 1 UNIT 01-04

UNIT 05   Can I bring my dog?

Key Patterns	Vocabulary	Useful Expressions	Goals
Can you come to my birthday party? Can I bring my dog?	my birthday party / my house / the concert / the picnic / the play / dog / friend / little brother / camera / hat / the school festival / the amusement park / the talent show / the baseball game	Hold on. Let me ask my mom. **Useful Question** Can Jack bring his dog?	• Inviting someone to certain events • Asking for permission with "can" ● Theme Inviting

UNIT 06   You must be quiet in here.

Key Patterns	Vocabulary	Useful Expression	Goals
You must be quiet in here. You must not shout in here.	be quiet / be on time / be careful / be polite / stop at the red light / wait in line / get enough sleep / shout / be late / run around / be rude / cross the street at the red light / cut in line / stay up late	I can't hear you! **Useful Questions** Pardon? What did you say?	• Talking about obligations and restrictions • Giving warnings ● Theme Warnings

UNIT 07   A coat is warmer than a jacket.

Key Patterns	Vocabulary	Useful Expressions	Goals
A coat is warmer than a jacket. A car is more comfortable than a train.	a jacket / a coat / warm - warmer / a hill / a mountain / high - higher / that hot dog / this sandwich / big - bigger / silver / gold / expensive - more expensive / a car / a train / fast - faster / comfortable - more comfortable / a river / a lake / small - smaller / a rock / a feather / light - lighter / a bear / an elephant / heavy - heavier / English / math / difficult - more difficult	Put on a coat. Slow down! Chew it well. **Useful Question** Is that a hill or a mountain?	• Comparing two things • Learning comparative forms ● Theme Taking a trip

UNIT 08   She's the tallest member.

Key Patterns	Vocabulary	Useful Expression	Goals
She's the tallest member. (I think) he's the most handsome member.	tall - taller - the tallest / woman / old - older - the oldest / man / young - younger - the youngest / child / strong - stronger - the strongest / boy / funny - funnier - the funniest / girl / popular - more popular - the most popular / singer / light - lighter - the lightest / bag / heavy - heavier - the heaviest / box / long - longer - the longest / snake / interesting - more interesting - the most interesting / book	I didn't know that. **Useful Questions** Are they singers? Who's the most handsome member?	• Making sentences using comparative/superlative adjectives • Expressing your own opinions ● Theme Favorite singing group

REVIEW TEST 2   UNIT 05-08

WORD LIST

A

amusement park	37

B

bag	55
balloon	21
banner	21
baseball game	37
be careful	41
be late	41
be on time	41
be polite	41
be quiet	41
be rude	41
beach umbrella	15
bear	49
big	47
bigger	47
birthday card	21
boardwalk	15
book	55
box	55
boy	53
building sandcastles	7
building snowmen	9
buying a present	25
buying shoes	27

C

cafe	13
camera	37
candle	21
car	47
cell phone	19
child	53
Chinese restaurant	27

D

clothing store	25
coat	47
collecting seashells	7
comfortable	47
concert	35
convenience store	13
cross the street at the red light	43
cut in line	43

difficult	49
diving	7
dog	35
drone	19

E

eighth	27
eighty	19
elephant	49
elevator	13
English	49
expensive	47

F

fast	47
fast food restaurant	13, 25
faster	47
feather	49
fifth	25
first	25
fourth	25
friend	35
funnier	53
funniest	53
funny	53

G

get enough sleep	43
gift shop	13
girl	53
going shopping	25
going to the theater	25
gold	47

H

hammock	15
hat	37
having a burger	25
having Chinese food	27
having snowball fights	9
heavier	49, 55
heaviest	55
heavy	49, 55
high	47
higher	47
hill	47
hot dog	47
hundred	19

I

ice skating	9
information center	13
interesting	55

J

jacket	47

K

kids baking school	27

VOCABULARY FLASHCARDS

UNIT 01

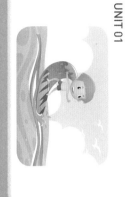
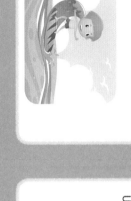

UNIT 01

UNIT 01

UNIT 02

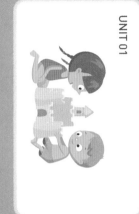

UNIT 01

UNIT 01

UNIT 01

UNIT 01

UNIT 01

UNIT 01

UNIT 01

UNIT 01

UNIT 01

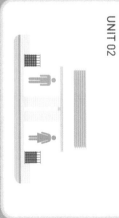

UNIT 01

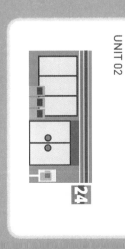

UNIT 02

24

swimming	surfing	sunbathing	diving
snorkeling	building sandcastles	collecting seashells	playing beach volleyball
building snowmen	having snowball fights	making snow angels	skiing
snowboarding	ice skating	the restroom	a convenience store

UNIT 02

UNIT 02

UNIT 02

UNIT 02

UNIT 02
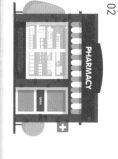
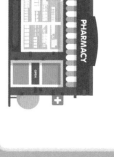

UNIT 02

UNIT 02

UNIT 03

UNIT 02

UNIT 02
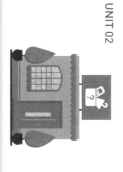

UNIT 02

UNIT 03

UNIT 02

UNIT 02

UNIT 03

UNIT 03

a gift shop

a fast food
restaurant

a sun chair

a palm tree

a pharmacy

the information
center

a beach umbrella

drone

an elevator

the lost-and-found
center

the boardwalk

cell phone

a cafe

a hammock

the lighthouse

mini fan

UNIT 03

$29.30
($50 for 2)

UNIT 03

70

UNIT 03

$3.50
($5 for 2)

UNIT 03

$26.54
($45 for 2)

UNIT 03

$139.99
($260 for 2)

UNIT 03

80

UNIT 03

$1.50
($2.40 for 2)

UNIT 03

$22.99
($36 for 2)

UNIT 03

$9.48
($18 for 2)

UNIT 03

90

UNIT 03

$4.98
($8 for 2)

UNIT 04

UNIT 03

60

UNIT 03

100

UNIT 03

$12.99
($20 for 2)

UNIT 04

THEATER

wireless mic	laptop	selfie stick	sixty
seventy	eighty	ninety	hundred
birthday card	balloon	candle	banner
mask	water gun	playing table tennis	going to the theater

UNIT 04

UNIT 04
2F

UNIT 04

UNIT 04

UNIT 04

UNIT 04
3F

UNIT 04

UNIT 04
CHINESE FOOD

UNIT 04

UNIT 04
BOX OFFICE
4F

UNIT 04

UNIT 04
LIBRARY

UNIT 04
BOX OFFICE

UNIT 04
5F

UNIT 04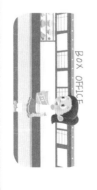
1F

having a burger	going shopping	buying a present	the first floor
the second floor	the third floor	the fourth floor	the fifth floor
toy shop	clothing store	fast food restaurant	theater
sports center	learning baking	having Chinese food	reading books

VOCABULARY FLASHCARDS

UNIT 04

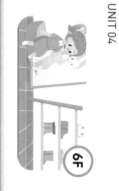

UNIT 04

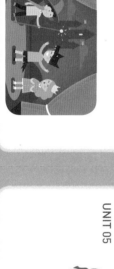
6F

UNIT 04

7F

UNIT 04

8F

UNIT 04

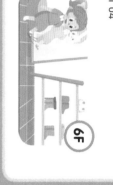
9F

UNIT 04

UNIT 04

UNIT 04

UNIT 05

UNIT 05

PARTY

UNIT 05

MY HOUSE

UNIT 05

UNIT 05

UNIT 05

UNIT 05

UNIT 05

buying shoes	the ninth floor	kids baking school	the picnic
the sixth floor	shoe store	my birthday party	the play
the seventh floor	library	my house	dog
the eighth floor	Chinese restaurant	the concert	friend

UNIT 06

UNIT 06

UNIT 06

UNIT 05

UNIT 05

UNIT 06

UNIT 06

UNIT 06

UNIT 06

UNIT 06

UNIT 06

UNIT 05

UNIT 05

UNIT 05

UNIT 05

the talent show

the amusement park

the school festival

little brother

be quiet

hat

camera

the baseball game

shout

be polite

be careful

be on time

stop at
the red light

be rude

run around

be late

VOCABULARY FLASHCARDS

UNIT 06

UNIT 06

UNIT 06

UNIT 06

UNIT 07

a rock / a feather

UNIT 07

silver / gold

UNIT 07

a jacket / a coat

UNIT 07

that hot dog / this sandwich

UNIT 07

a bear / an elephant

UNIT 07

a car / a train

UNIT 07

a hill / a mountain

UNIT 07

a river / a lake

UNIT 07

English / math

Do you speak English?

4140÷200
= 72
X = 1

???

UNIT 07

a train / a car

UNIT 06

UNIT 08

cut in line

cross the street at the red light

get enough sleep

wait in line

stay up late

expensive - more expensive

light - lighter

warm - warmer

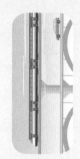

fast - faster

heavy - heavier

high - higher

comfortable - more comfortable

difficult - more difficult

big - bigger

small – smaller

tall - taller - the tallest woman

UNIT 08

UNIT 08

UNIT 08

UNIT 08

UNIT 08

UNIT 08

UNIT 08

UNIT 08

UNIT 08

old - older - the oldest
man

popular - more popular
- the most popular
singer

interesting
- more interesting
- the most interesting
book

young - younger
- the youngest
child

light - lighter
- the lightest
bag

strong - stronger
- the strongest
boy

heavy - heavier
- the heaviest
box

funny - funnier
- the funniest
girl

long - longer
- the longest
snake

UNIT 03

How much is that

UNIT 02

I'm looking for

UNIT 01

best

UNIT 01

I enjoy

UNIT 03

It's

UNIT 03

How much is this

UNIT 02

Where can I find

UNIT 01

I like

UNIT 03

It's ____ for one
and ____ for two.

UNIT 04

It's on

UNIT 05

Can I bring my

UNIT 06

You must not

UNIT 04

How about

UNIT 05

Can you come to

UNIT 06

You must

UNIT 07

is warmer than

UNIT 07

is higher than

UNIT 07

is more expensive than

UNIT 07

is more comfortable than

UNIT 07

is lighter than

UNIT 07

is bigger than

UNIT 07

is faster than

UNIT 07

is smaller than

UNIT 07

is heavier than

UNIT 07

is more difficult than

UNIT 08

She's

UNIT 08

I think she's

UNIT 08

It's

UNIT 08

He's

UNIT 08

I think he's

UNIT 08

This is

UNIT 08

I think this is

UNIT 08

I think it's

UNIT 08

among them

with 세이펜

원어민 음성을 실시간 반복학습	단어 및 대화의 우리말 해석 듣기	선생님의 Workbook Guide로 혼자서도 쉽게 학습

세이펜 핀파일 다운로드 안내

STEP ① 세이펜과 컴퓨터를 USB 케이블로 연결하세요.

STEP ② 쎄듀북 홈페이지(www.cedubook.com)에 접속 후, 학습자료실 메뉴에서 학습할 교재를 찾아 이동합니다.

> 초등교재 ▶ ELT ▶ 학습교재 클릭 ▶ 세이쎈 핀파일 자료 클릭
> ▶ 다운로드 (저장을 '다른 이름으로 저장'으로 변경하여 저장소를 USB로 변경) ▶ 완료

STEP ③ 음원 다운로드가 완료되면 세이펜과 컴퓨터의 USB 케이블을 분리하세요.

STEP ④ 세이펜을 분리하면 "시스템을 초기화 중입니다. 잠시만 기다려 주세요." 라는 멘트가 나옵니다.

STEP ⑤ 멘트 종료 후 세이펜을 〈Oh! My Speaking〉 표지에 대보세요.
효과음이 나온 후 바로 학습을 시작할 수 있습니다.

참고사항

◆ 세이펜은 본 교재에 포함되어 있지 않습니다. 별도로 구매하여 이용할 수 있으며, 기존에 보유하신 세이펜이 있다면 핀파일만 다운로드해서
바로 이용하실 수 있습니다.

◆ 세이펜에서 제작된 모든 기종(기존에 보유하고 계신 기종도 호환 가능)으로 사용이 가능합니다.

◆ 모든 기종은 세이펜에서 권장하는 최신 펌웨어 업데이트를 진행해 주시기 바랍니다.
업데이트는 세이펜 홈페이지(www.saypen.com)에서 가능합니다.

◆ 핀파일은 쎄듀북 홈페이지(www.cedubook.com)와 세이펜 홈페이지(www.saypen.com)에서 모두 다운로드 가능합니다.

◆ 세이펜을 이용하지 않는 학습자는 쎄듀북 홈페이지 부가학습자료, 교재 내 QR코드 이미지 등을 활용하여 원어민 음성으로 학습하실 수 있습니다.

◆ 기타 문의사항은 www.cedubook.com / 02-3272-4766으로 연락 바랍니다.

세이펜과 함께 배우는 Oh! My Speaking

〈Oh! My Speaking〉은 세이펜이 적용된 도서입니다. 세이펜을 가져다 대면 원어민의 생생한 영어 발음과 억양을 듣고 영어 말하기 연습을 할 수 있습니다.
*번역 기능 | 세이펜으로 책을 찍어서 원어민 음성을 들은 후, T 버튼을 짧게 누르면 우리말 해석 음원을 들을 수 있습니다.

✏ 세이펜을 대면 유닛명을 들을 수 있습니다. T 기능 지원

✏ QR코드에 세이펜을 대면 해당 MP3파일이 재생됩니다.

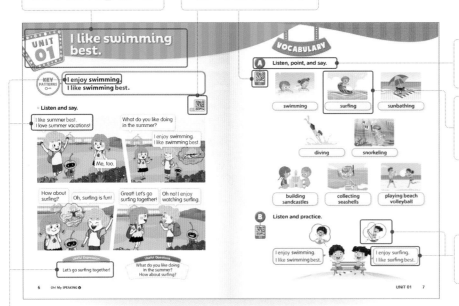

✏ 세이펜을 대면 Activity의 지시문을 들을 수 있습니다. T 기능 지원

✏ 그림이나 영어 단어에 세이펜을 대면 원어민의 발음을 들을 수 있습니다. T 기능 지원

✏ 그림이나 말풍선에 세이펜을 대면 해당 문장을 들을 수 있습니다. T 기능 지원

✏ 영어 문장에 세이펜을 대면 원어민의 정확한 발음과 억양을 들을 수 있습니다. T 기능 지원

✏ 번호에 세이펜을 대면 해당 그림에 대한 Key Pattern 대화가 재생되며, 그림이나 영어 단어에 세이펜을 대면 해당 영어 단어를 들을 수 있습니다. T 기능 지원

✏ 영어 문장이나 단어에 세이펜을 대면 원어민의 정확한 발음과 억양을 들을 수 있습니다. T 기능 지원

✏ 그림에 세이펜을 대면 해당 그림에 대한 Key Pattern 대화를 들을 수 있습니다. T 기능 지원

✏ 문제 번호에 세이펜을 대면 해당 문제의 음원이 재생되며, 말풍선에 세이펜을 대면 해당 문장 또는 정답 영어 문장을 들을 수 있습니다. T 기능 지원

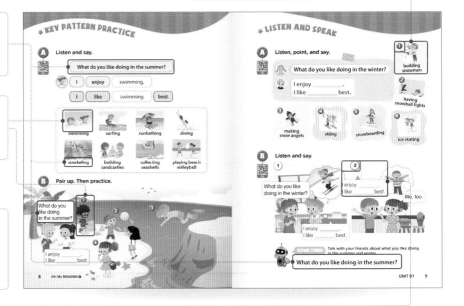

WORKBOOK

Oh! My SPEAKING

6

with SAYPEN

MP3 CD Included

SAYPEN
www.saypen.com
SAY GO

CEDU BOOK

oh! MY SPEAKING 6

WORKBOOK

CEDU BOOK

UNIT 01 I like swimming best.

A Look and write. Use the hints from the cue box.

(HELP)

1

2

3

4

5

6

Cue Box

skiing	sunbathing	diving
ice skating	snowboarding	swimming

B Look and complete the sentences.

(HELP)

1

I enjoy surfing.

I like s_____ best.

2

I enjoy building sandcastles.

I like b_____ s_____ best.

3

I enjoy making snow angels.

I like m_____ s_____ a_____ best.

C Trace, unscramble, and write.

HELP

1

 What do you like doing in the summer?

enjoy / snorkeling / I / .

like / snorkeling / I / best / .

2

I / collecting / enjoy / seashells / .

collecting / I / best / like / seashells / .

Me, too.

3

 What do you like doing in the winter?

having / I / snowball fights / enjoy / .

like / best / snowball fights / having / I / .

4

snowmen / enjoy / I / building / .

building / like / I / best / snowmen / .

Me, too.

D Listen and write O if the dialogue and the picture match, and X if they don't.

1

2

3

4

E Listen and choose the right sentence for the blank.

1

 What do you like doing in the summer?

ⓐ　　ⓑ　　ⓒ

2

 What do you like doing in the winter?

ⓐ　　ⓑ　　ⓒ

F Put the dialogue in the correct order.
Then listen to it and practice with a friend.

Amy: What do you like doing in the summer?

Jack: I enjoy swimming. I like swimming best.

Jack: Oh, surfing is fun!

Amy: How about surfing?

Amy: Great! Let's go surfing together!

Jack: Oh no! I enjoy watching surfing.

YOUR TURN! What do you like doing in the summer and winter?
Choose and complete the sentences.

I enjoy _____ .

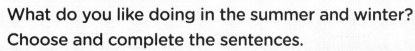
I like _____ best.

I enjoy _____ .

I like _____ best.

UNIT 02 Where can I find the restroom?

A Write and find the words.

HELP

1

2

3

4

5

6

d	s	o	b	r	t	u	r	j	c
a	c	a	f	e	g	z	t	s	e
k	a	s	n	s	x	k	z	v	l
l	i	g	h	t	h	o	u	s	e
i	t	d	b	r	c	n	k	e	v
n	o	a	z	o	w	e	r	q	a
g	r	t	n	o	x	t	g	u	t
e	h	a	m	m	o	c	k	e	o
x	z	w	q	s	b	k	n	y	r
b	o	a	r	d	w	a	l	k	c

B Look and complete the sentences.

HELP

1  **A:** I'm looking for a p_____.

   B: It's around the corner.

2   **A:** Where can I find a g_____ s_____?

   B: It's over there.

3   **A:** I'm looking for a s_____ c_____.

   B: It's around the corner.

C  **Trace, unscramble, and write.**

HELP ✏

1

 Excuse me.

_____

palm tree / I'm / a / looking for / .

It's over there.

2

Excuse me.

_____

can / find / Where / a / I / fast food restaurant / ?

It's around the corner.

3

Excuse me.

_____

looking for / a / I'm / beach umbrella / .

It's over there.

4

Excuse me.

_____

find / Where / I / the / can / information center / ?

It's around the corner.

D Listen and write O if the dialogue and the picture match, and X if they don't.

1
CAFE
OPEN

2
24

3
?

4

E Listen and choose the right sentence for the blank.

1

_____.

It's around the corner.

a   b   c

2

_____?

It's over there.

a   b   c

F **Put the dialogue in the correct order.**
Then listen to it and practice with a friend.

Wacky: Oh, my battery is low!

Jack: You should recharge it.

Manager: It's over there.

Wacky: Thank you.

Wacky: Excuse me.
I'm looking for a charging station.

Jack: Wacky, where are you?

Wacky: Jack, I'm here. I'm full.

   What are you looking for? Complete the sentences.

A: I'm looking for a/an _____.

B: It's over there.

A: Where can I find a/an _____?

B: It's around the corner.

How much is this?

A Fill in the blanks below each picture to complete the word.

HELP

1 __ ap __ __ __

2 __ __ ll __ __ __ ne

3 __ __ o __ __ __

4 __ a __ __ er

5 __ an __ __ __ __

6 __ __ ll __ __ n

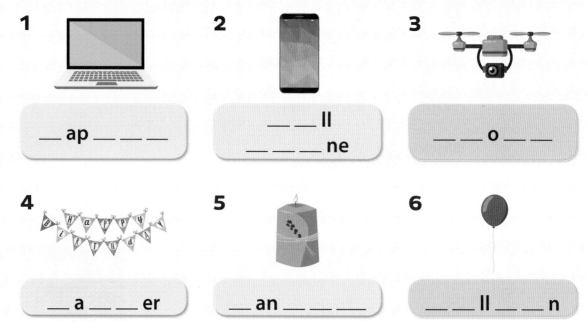

B Look and complete the sentences.

HELP

1 $9.48 ($18 for 2)

A: How much is this s _____ s _____ ?

B: It's $9.48.

2 HAPPY BIRTHDAY $3.50 ($5 for 2)

A: How much is that b _____ c _____ ?

B: It's $3.50.

3 $22.99 ($36 for 2)

A: How much is that w _____ g _____ ?

B: It's $22.99 for one and $36 for two.

C Trace, unscramble, and write.

HELP

1

_____
this / is / How much / wireless mic / ?

 It's $29.30.

2

_____
is / How much / mini fan / that / ?

 It's $10.99 for one and $16 for two.

3

_____
banner / this / How much / is / ?

 It's $12.99.

4

 How much is that mask?

_____
for one / It's / $26.54 / and / for two / $45 / .

D Listen and write O if the dialogue and the picture match, and X if they don't.

85
HELP

1

$78

2

$15.30
($25 for 2)

How much is this
_____?

3

$99.99

4

$12
($20 for 2)

How much is that
_____?

E Listen and choose the right sentence for the blank.

86
HELP

1

$25 $26

How much is this mask?

_____.

a   **b**   **c**

2

$3.50
($6 for 2)

CARDS

_____?

It's $3.50 for one and $6 for two.

a   **b**   **c**

F **Put the dialogue in the correct order.
Then listen to it and practice with a friend.**

Jack: I want a new drone. How much is this?

Wacky: It's $100.

Jack: I only have $30. How much is that drone?

Wacky: It's $40 for one and $70 for two.

Mom: If you clean your room, I'll give you $10.

Jack: Yay! I'll clean my room right now!

YOUR TURN! How much is this? Choose and complete the sentences.

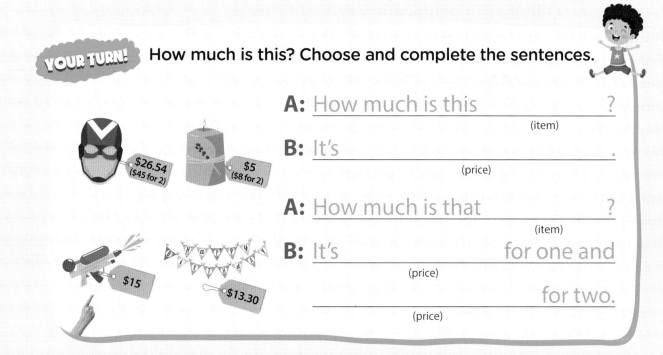

A: How much is this _____ ?
_____ (item)

B: It's _____ .
_____ (price)

A: How much is that _____ ?
_____ (item)

B: It's _____ for one and
_____ (price)

_____ for two.
_____ (price)

$26.54
($45 for 2)

$5
($8 for 2)

$15

$13.30

How about playing table tennis?

A What are they doing? Unscramble and write the words.

(HELP)

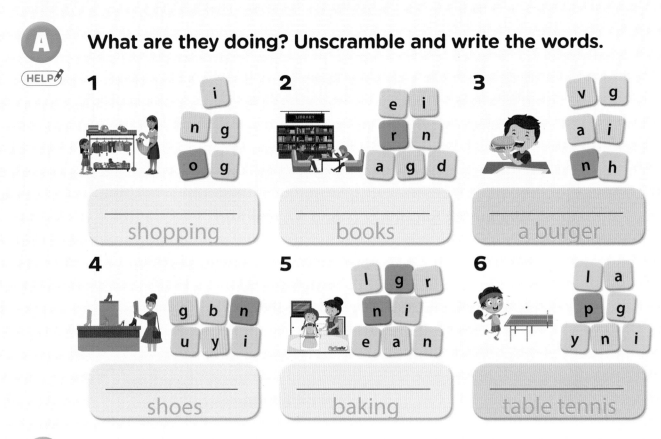

1 _____ shopping

2 _____ books

3 _____ a burger

4 _____ shoes

5 _____ baking

6 _____ table tennis

B Look and complete the sentences.

(HELP)

1 **A:** How about b_____ a present?

   B: Sounds good.

2 **A:** Where's the fast food restaurant?

   B: It's on the f_____ floor.

3 **A:** How about g_____ to the theater?

   B: Okay. Where's the theater?

   A: It's on the f_____ floor.

C Trace, unscramble, and write.

(HELP)

1
_____
Chinese food / How about / having / ?

 Sounds good. _____

2  Where's the library? _____

 _____
the seventh floor / on / It's /.

3
_____
learning / baking / How about / ?

 Sounds good. _____

4  Where's the sports center? _____

 _____
on / It's / the fifth floor / .

D Listen and write O if the dialogue and the picture match, and X if they don't.

1

2

the second floor
clothing store

3

the sixth floor
shoe store

4

E Listen and choose the right sentence for the blank.

1

the ninth floor
kids baking school

Where's the kids baking school?

a b c

2

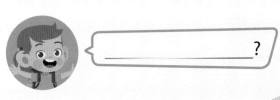

?

Sounds good.

a b c

90

HELP

F **Put the dialogue in the correct order.**
Then listen to it and practice with a friend.

Tom: How about playing table tennis tomorrow?

Jack: Sounds good.

Jack: Okay. Where do you want to meet?

Tom: How about having lunch before the game?

Tom: Let's meet at King's Burger.
It's on the second floor of that building.

Jack: Okay, I see it. See you there at 12.

Make a suggestion to your friend.
Complete the sentences.

A: How about _____ ?

B: Sounds good.

Where's the _____ ?

A: It's on the _____ floor.

the fifth floor sports center

the fourth floor theater

the third floor fast food restaurant

the second floor clothing store

the first floor toy shop

UNIT 05 Can I bring my dog?

A Look and write. Use the hints from the cue box.

HELP

1

2

3

4

5

6

Cue Box	amusement park	play	school festival
	picnic	concert	talent show

B Look and complete the sentences.

HELP

1

A: Can you come to my b_____ p_____?

B: Sure.

2

A: Can you come to the b_____ g_____?

B: Sure. Thanks.

3

A: Can you come to my h_____?

B: Sure. Can I bring my d_____?

A: Okay.

Trace, unscramble, and write.

HELP

1

_____

come / Can / to the talent show / you / ?

Sure. Thanks. _____

2

_____

Can / come / you / to the play / ?

Sure. Thanks. _____

3

_____

to the concert / you / come / Can / ?

Sure. Thanks. _____

4

_____

you / come / Can / to the amusement park / ?

Sure. _____

bring / Can / my camera / I / ?

Okay. _____

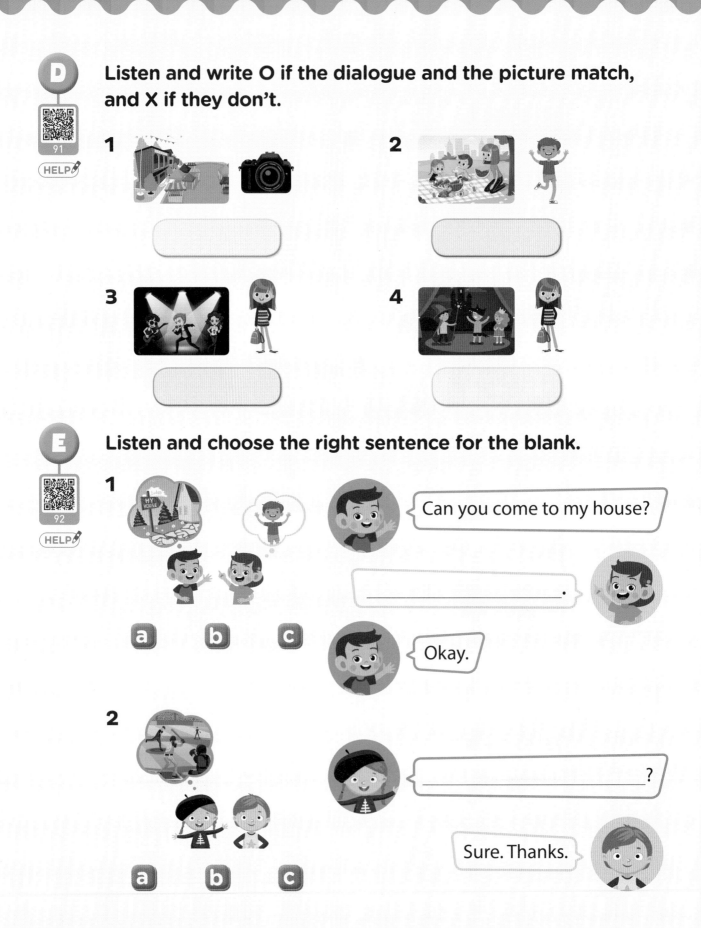

D Listen and write O if the dialogue and the picture match, and X if they don't.

1

2

3

4

E Listen and choose the right sentence for the blank.

1

a   b   c

Can you come to my house?

_____.

Okay.

2

a   b   c

_____?

Sure. Thanks.

F Put the dialogue in the correct order.
Then listen to it and practice with a friend.

Amy: Hold on. Let me ask my mom. ☐

Jack: Sure. Thanks. Can I bring my dog? ☐

Amy: Can you come to my birthday party on Saturday? ☐

Amy: Mom, can Jack bring his dog?

Amy's Mom: Sure.

Amy: You can bring your dog.

Jack: Great! See you on Saturday.

YOUR TURN! Invite your friend to the event.
Look and complete the sentences.

A: Can you come to

_____ ?

B: Sure. Thanks.
Can I bring my _____ ?

A: Yes, you can. /
No, you can't. I'm sorry.

UNIT 06 You must be quiet in here.

A What are they like? Write and find the words.

HELP

1

be _____

4

be _____

2

be _____

5

_____

3

_____ in line

6

_____ in line

w	o	f	x	r	d	b	m	y	r
a	a	c	s	n	b	x	q	z	u
c	g	i	g	h	f	r	u	d	e
e	h	g	t	n	u	s	i	k	h
h	d	b	a	z	o	w	e	r	c
t	c	d	p	o	l	i	t	e	l
k	m	d	r	t	o	s	k	h	s
f	h	a	h	a	c	g	x	b	d
x	z	w	q	s	u	d	n	r	p
t	s	h	o	u	t	t	g	u	z

B Look and complete the sentences.

HELP

1 You must not s_____ up l_____.

2 You must s_____ at the r_____ l_____.

3 You must not r_____ a_____.

Trace, unscramble, and write.

1

I want to take pictures.

_____

not / take pictures / You / must / in here / .

2

Hey! Come over here!

_____

must / You / in the library / be quiet / .

3

I'm sorry. I'm late.

_____

be late / must / You / not / .

4

Uh oh.

_____

on the wet floor / be careful / must / You / .

D Listen and number.

E What would you say to them?
Listen and choose the right sentence for the blank.

1

You must _____.

2

You must not _____.

F Put the dialogue in the correct order.
Then listen to it and practice with a friend.

Jack: I want to take pictures.

Security Guard: Excuse me.
You must not take pictures in here.

Jack: Pardon? What did you say?

Security Guard: You must not shout in here.

Jack: I can't hear you!

Security Guard: You must be quiet
in here!

YOUR TURN! What are rules here? Look and complete the sentences.

You must not _____ .

You must _____ .

UNIT 07
A coat is warmer than a jacket.

A **Compare the two. Fill in the blanks below each picture to complete the word.**

(HELP)

1

__ i __ __ er

2

hi __ __ __ __ __

3

h __ __ __ __ __ er

4

more

__ i __ i __ __ lt

5

more

c __ __ __ or __ able

6

more

e __ __ en __ __ ve

B **Look and complete the sentences.**

(HELP)

1

A m_____ is h_____ than a hill.

2

A f_____ is l_____ than a rock.

3

Gold is m_____ e_____ than silver.

Trace, unscramble, and write.

HELP

1

warmer / A coat / is / a jacket / than / .

2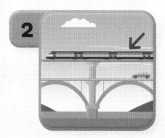

is / than / faster / a car / A train / .

3

than / is / This sandwich / bigger / that hot dog / .

4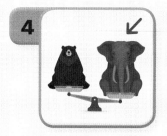

An elephant / a bear / heavier / than / is / .

5

than / Math / more difficult / English / is / .

D Listen and number.

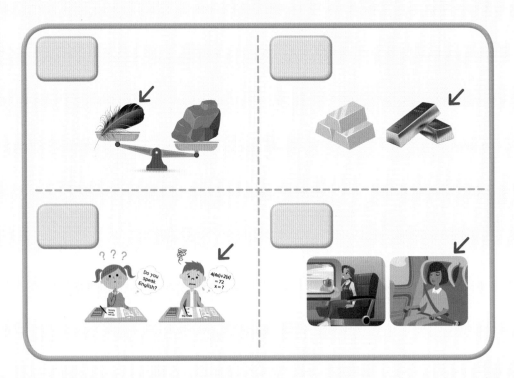

E Listen and choose the right sentence for the blank.

1

An elephant is _____.

a b c

2

A car is _____.

a b c

99

HELP

F Put the dialogue in the correct order.
Then listen to it and practice with a friend.

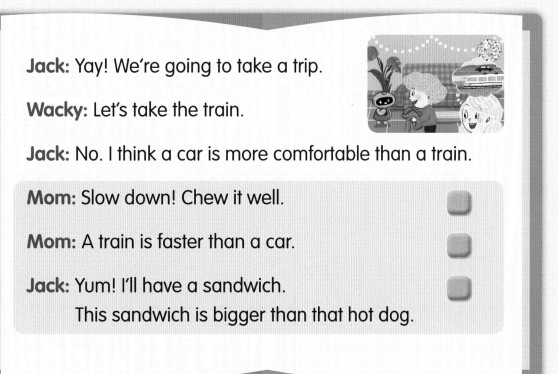

Jack: Yay! We're going to take a trip.

Wacky: Let's take the train.

Jack: No. I think a car is more comfortable than a train.

Mom: Slow down! Chew it well.

Mom: A train is faster than a car.

Jack: Yum! I'll have a sandwich.
This sandwich is bigger than that hot dog.

YOUR TURN! Compare the two items using comparative forms.

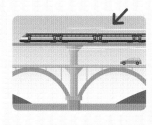

(a train, fast, a car)

_____

(a lake, small, a river)

_____

She's the tallest member.

A Unscramble and write the words.

HELP

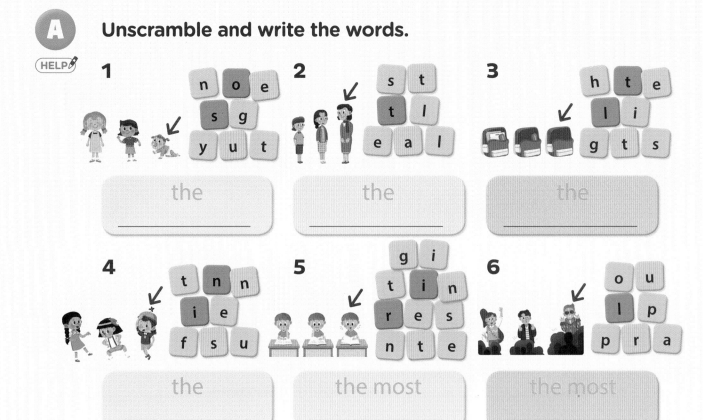

1 the _____

2 the _____

3 the _____

4 the _____

5 the most _____

6 the most _____

B Look and complete the sentences.

HELP

1 He's the s _____ boy.

2 She's the t _____ woman.

3 It's the l _____ snake.

C Trace, unscramble, and write.

HELP

1

Mr. Kim   Mr. Lee   Mr. Park

man / the / Mr. Park / oldest / is / .

2

Pam   Wendy   Mary

child / youngest / the / Mary / is / .

3

the / is / heaviest / box / The red box / .

4

is / The green bag / lightest / the / bag / .

5

Peter Pan

I think

is / the / book / most interesting / *Peter Pan* / .

D Let's compare. Listen and number.

E Listen and choose the right sentence for the blank.

1

Who's the oldest man?

 a   b   c

2

a   b   c

102

HELP

F **Put the dialogue in the correct order.**
Then listen to it and practice with a friend.

Amy: I like BGS! They're the most popular singing group in the world!

Jack: Oh, I didn't know that.

Amy: Look! She's the tallest member.

Jack: Who's the most handsome member?

Amy: I think he's the most handsome member.

Jack: Wow, she's really tall!

YOUR TURN! Compare the three children using superlative forms.

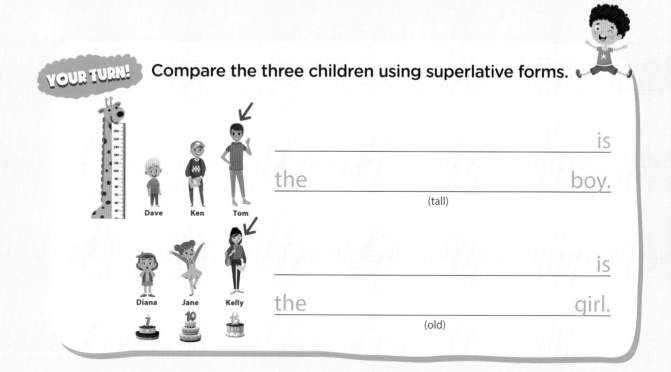

_____ is
the _____ boy.
       (tall)

_____ is
the _____ girl.
       (old)

WORKBOOK GUIDE

- Try to do the workbook activities on your own as much as possible.
- If you need additional help or want to hear the answers, scan the appropriate QR code below using your phone.
- You will be able to listen to the teacher's explanation immediately!

A **B** **C** **D** **E** **F**

UNIT 02

A **B** **C** **D** **E** **F**

UNIT 03

A **B** **C** **D** **E** **F**

UNIT 04

A **B** **C** **D** **E** **F**

UNIT 05

A   B   C   D   E   F

UNIT 06

A   B   C   D   E   F

UNIT 07

A   B   C   D   E   F

UNIT 08

A   B   C   D   E   F

Oh! My Speaking is a six-level speaking series designed for young learners. With task-based activities and vivid illustrations, *Oh! My Speaking* allows students to build up their confidence in speaking and to communicate with their peers in fun and interesting ways. By focusing on basic key words and key patterns with *Oh! My Speaking*, students set out on the journey toward becoming strong speakers of English.

Oh! My Speaking Series

SAYCODE II SAYPEN
Oh! My Speaking
SD4-OHMS

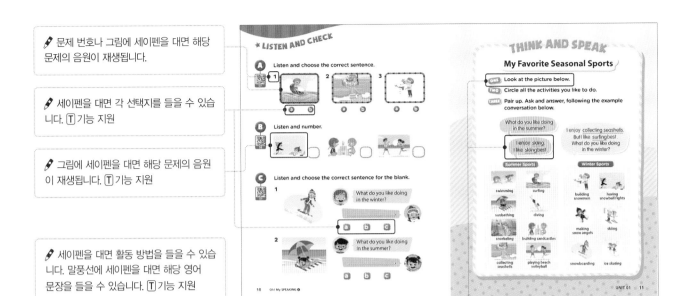

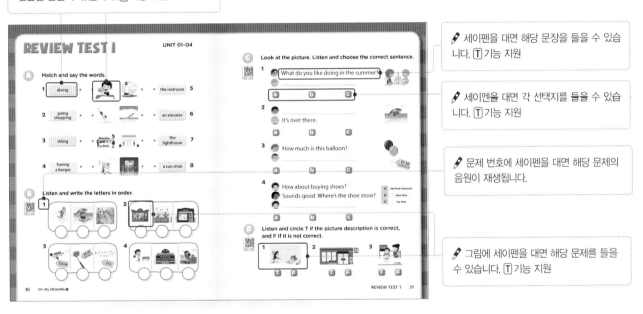

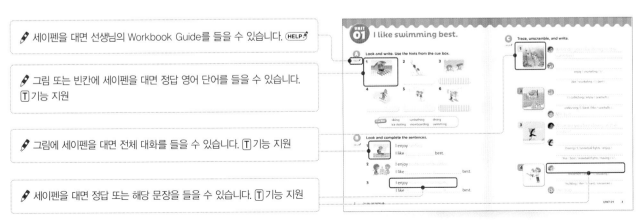

클래스가 다른~

Oh! My SPEAKING
Online Study
클래스 카드

CLASS CARD

완벽한 예습·복습을 위한 **온라인 무료 학습 시스템**

· PC(크롬) 또는 모바일앱 중 편리한 기기 선택
· 음성인식 서비스로 말하기 완결성 확인
· 단어 매칭게임 및 테스트 시험지 생성
· 원어민 음성으로 문장과 단어 말하기 연습
· 녹음 제출 기능으로 선생님과 학부모에게 결과 공유
· 선생님이 학부모에게 카톡으로 녹음 파일 전송 가능

1 문장 SPEAKING 학습(원어민 음성)

1. 스피킹 학습설정

2. 문장 뜻 파악

3. 반복 듣기

4. 큰소리로 읽기

5. 외워서 말하기

2 단어 암기 학습

1. 단어 확인&암기

2. 매칭 게임&단어 테스트

3 문장 암기 학습

1. 문장 뜻, 발음 확인&암기

2. 리콜 학습&스크램블 게임

* 서비스의 자세한 사용 방법은 쎄듀북 홈페이지(www.cedubook.com)를 확인해 주시기 바랍니다.

* 본 서비스는 제휴사와의 서비스 계약에 따라 예고없이 종료될 수 있습니다.

클래스 카드 ▼

학습하러 가기